Trace the numbers.

P9-DFX-519

0 1 2 3 4

5 6 7 8 9

10 11 12 13

14 15 16 17

18 19 20

SCHOOL BUS

Trace and write the numbers.

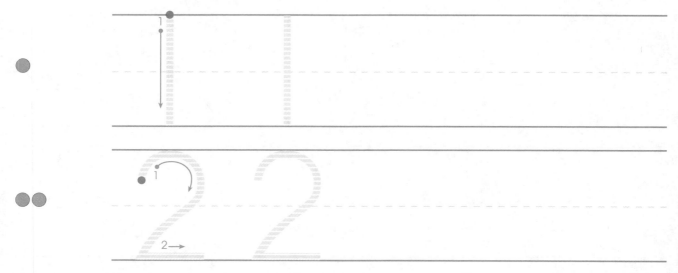

How many animals are there?
Write the number.

Draw a line to match each group to the correct number.

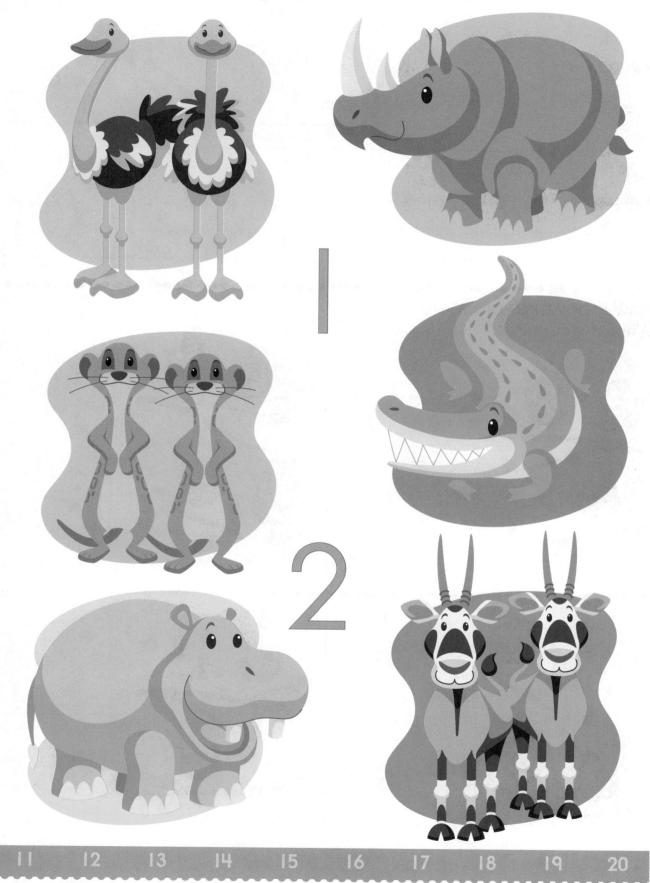

3
Learning about the Numbers 1 and 2 (K.CC.4.a,b,c)

Trace and write the numbers.

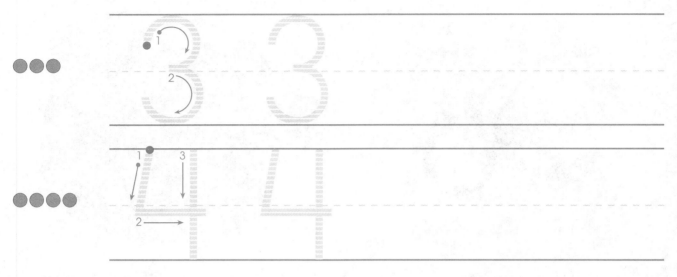

How many birds are there?
Write the number.

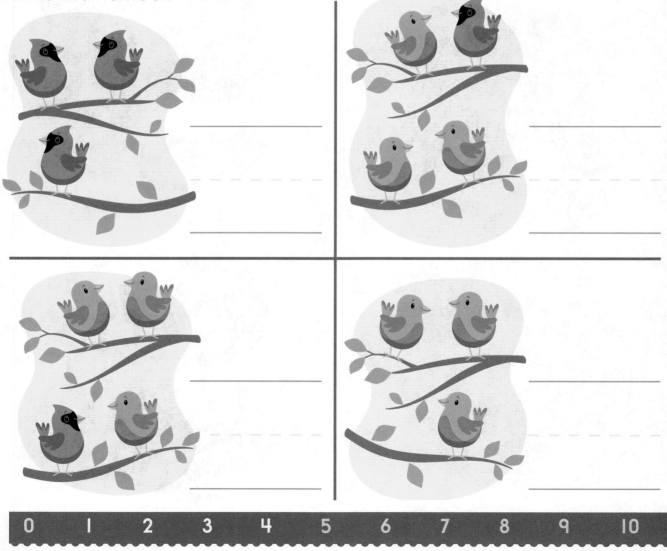

0 1 2 3 4 5 6 7 8 9 10

Color **1** chick **red**.

Color **2** chicks **orange**.

Color **3** chicks **blue**.

Color **4** chicks **yellow**.

5

Learning about the Numbers 3 and 4 (K.CC.5)

Trace and write the number zero.

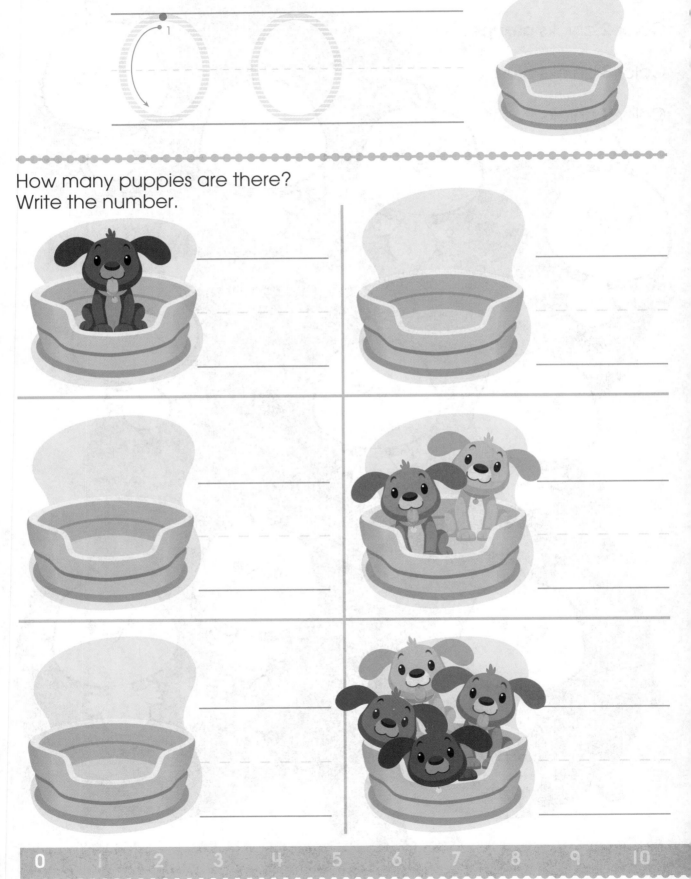

How many puppies are there?
Write the number.

Check the areas that have **0** kittens.

Trace and write the numbers.

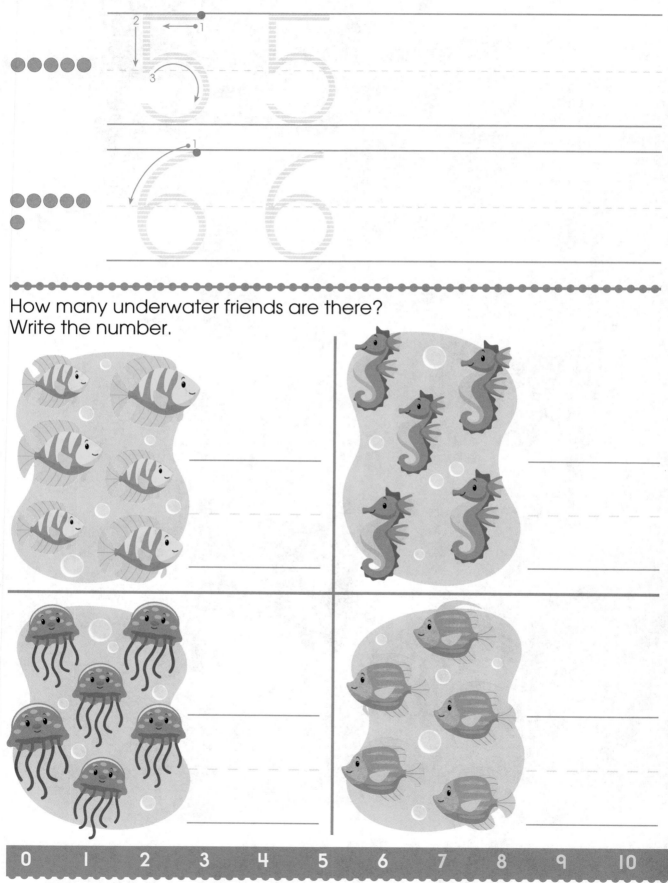

How many underwater friends are there?
Write the number.

0 1 2 3 4 5 6 7 8 9 10

Count each group.
Circle the number.

4   5   6

4   5   6

4   5   6

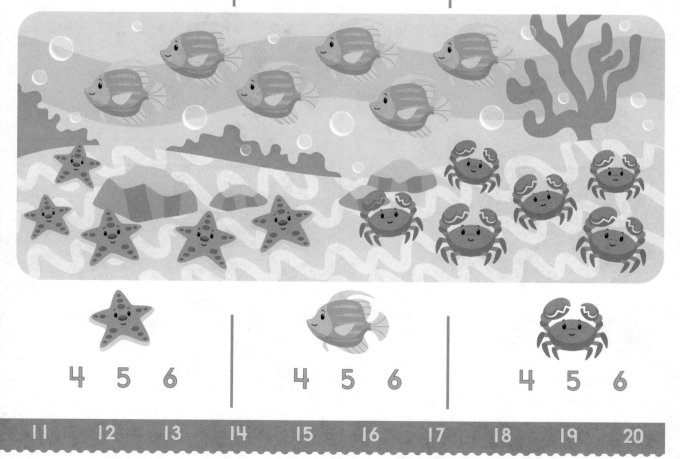

4   5   6   4   5   6   4   5   6

Learning about the Numbers 5 and 6 (K.CC.5)

Trace and write the numbers.

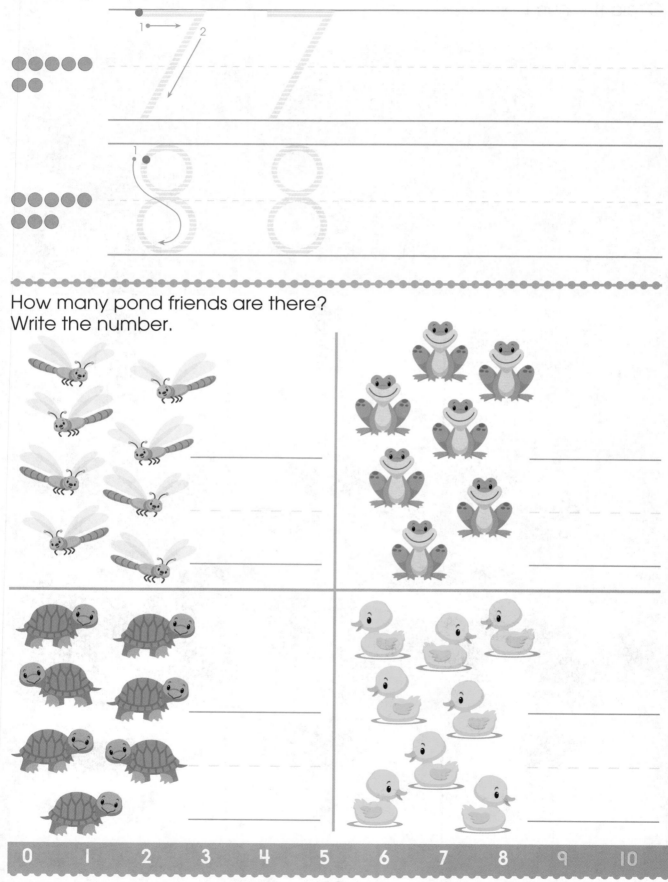

How many pond friends are there?
Write the number.

| 0 | 1 | 2 | 3 | 4 | 5 | 6 | 7 | 8 | 9 | 10 |

Count each group.
Write the number.

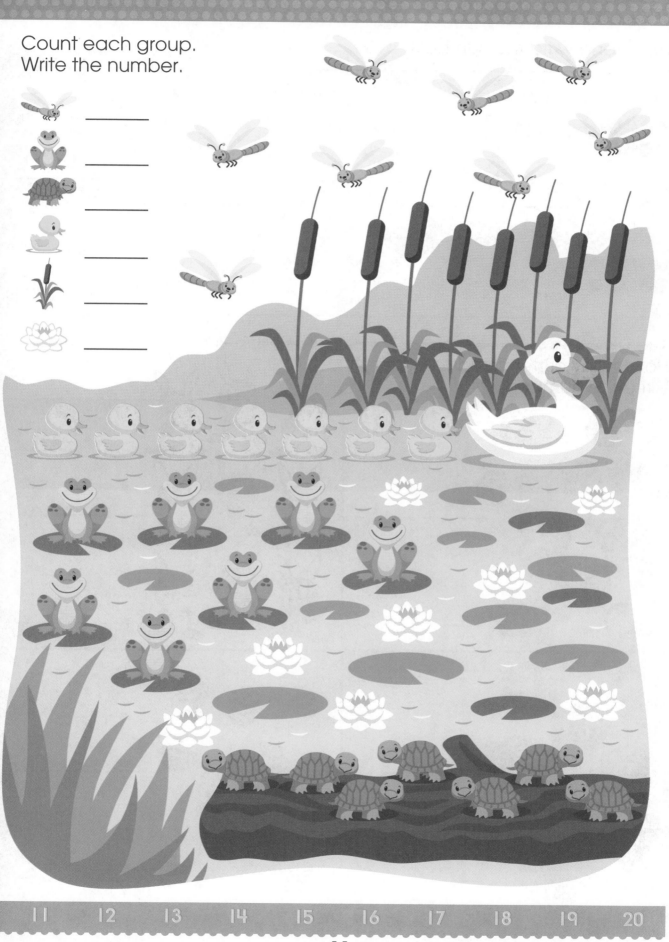

Learning about the Numbers 7 and 8 (K.CC.2,3,5)

Trace and write the numbers.

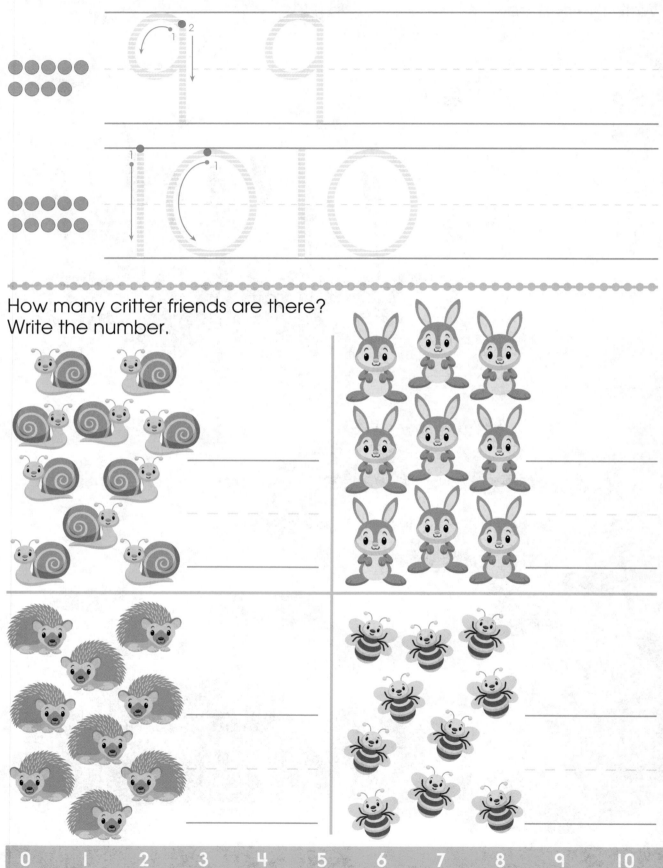

How many critter friends are there?
Write the number.

Count each group.
Write the number.

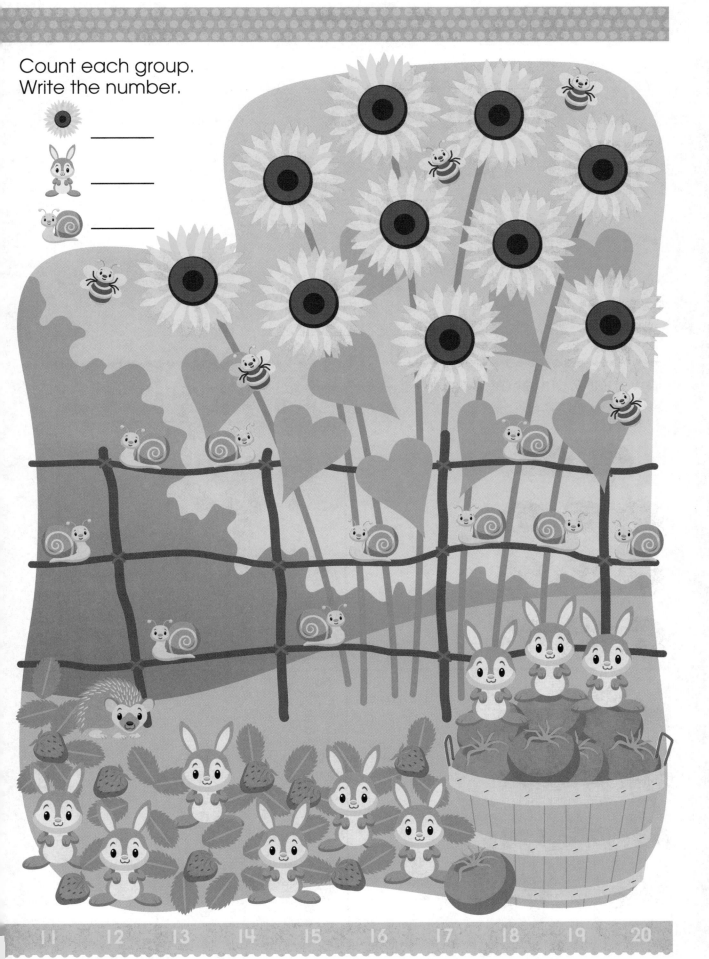

13 Learning about the Numbers 9 and 10 (K.CC.2,3,5)

Trace and write the numbers.

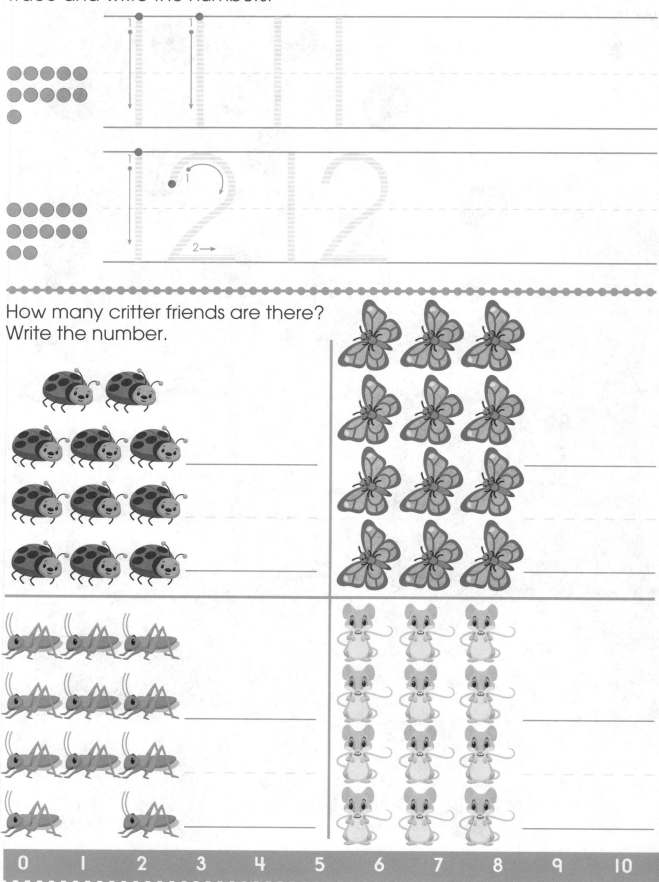

How many critter friends are there?
Write the number.

0	1	2	3	4	5	6	7	8	9	10

Write the number of  . _____

Write the number of . _____

Write the number of . _____

15   Learning about the Numbers 11 and 12 (K.CC.2,3,4)

Match the numbers to the vegetables.

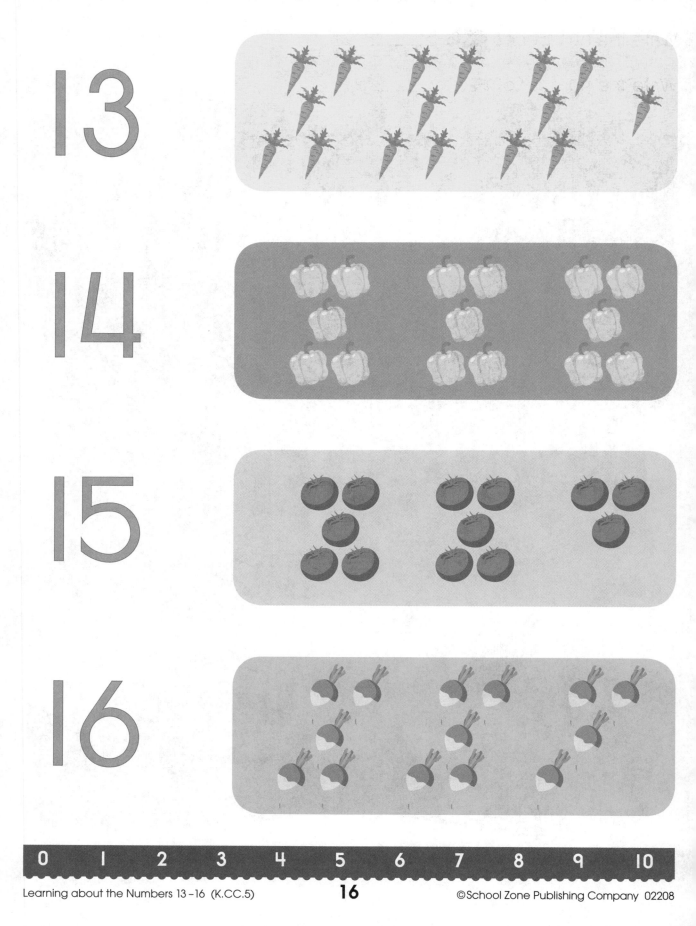

13

14

15

16

Learning about the Numbers 13–16 (K.CC.5)

16

©School Zone Publishing Company 02208

Match the numbers to the fruit.

17

18

19

20

| 11 | 12 | 13 | 14 | 15 | 16 | 17 | 18 | 19 | 20 |

Learning about the Numbers 17–20 (K.CC.5)

The number **11** comes **before** the number **12**.

Write the number that comes **before**.

19 20

14 15

17 18

11 12

16 17

13 14

Fishing For Numbers

The number **17** comes **after** the number **16**.

Write the number that comes **after**.

11 12

18 19

17 18

13 14

10 11

14 15

©School Zone Publishing Company 02208

Practicing Numerical Order: Concept of After (K.CC.3)

The number **14** comes **between** the numbers **13** and **15**.

Write the number that comes **between**.

Fruit Salad

Read the numbers. Draw the missing pieces of fruit.

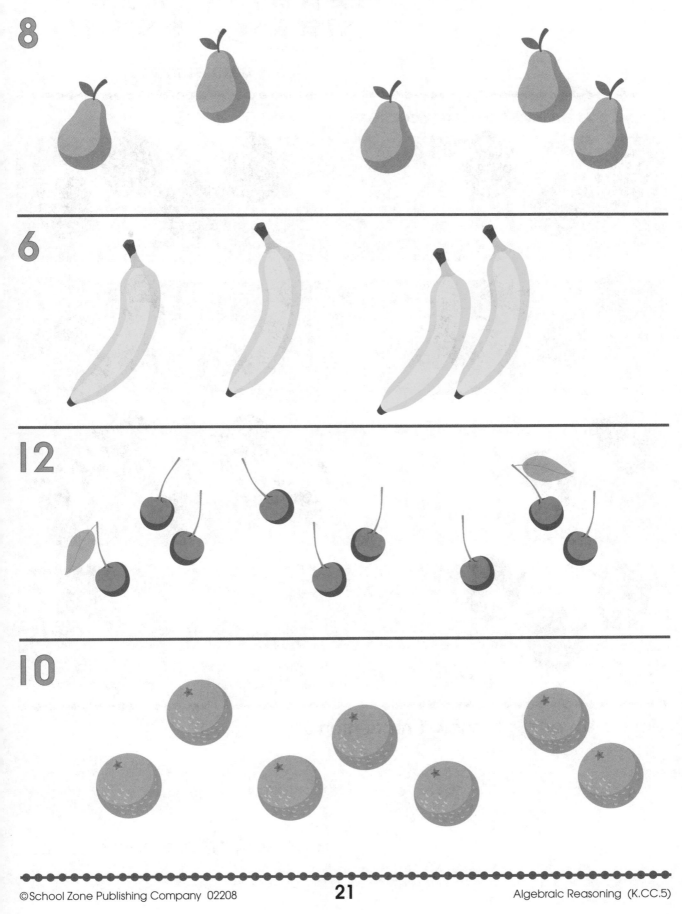

8

6

12

10

Algebraic Reasoning (K.CC.5)

Greater means **more than**.

8 is **greater than** 7.

Circle the groups that are **greater**.

Make a set of ⭐ to show **1 more than 3**.

How many ⭐ are there? _____

Less means **not as many**.

8 is **less than** 9.

Circle the groups that have **less**.

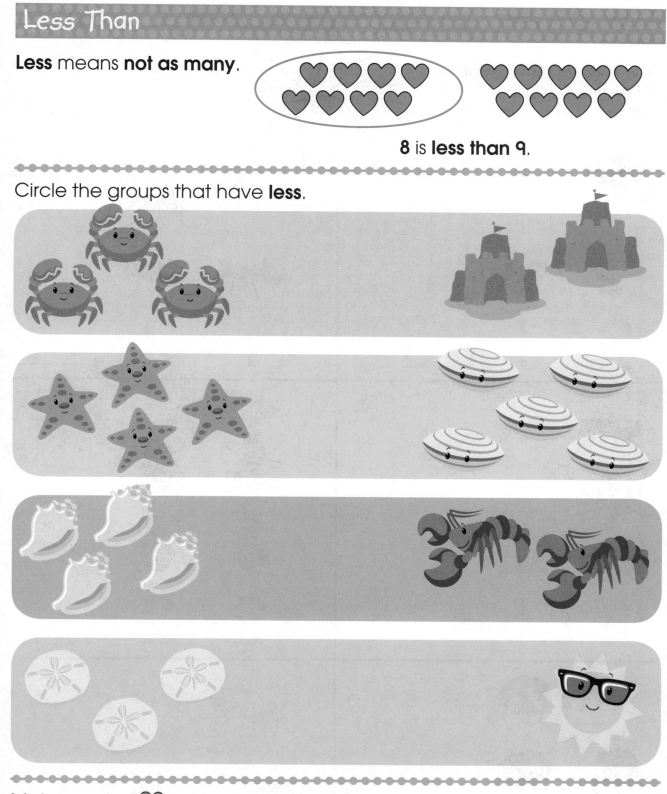

Make a set of ♥ to show **1 less than 3**.

How many ♥ are there? _____

23

Learning To Add With Bugs

How many are there **in all**?
Write the number.
The first one is done for you.

$2 + 1 = \underline{3}$

$1 + 2 = \underline{}$

$3 + 1 = \underline{}$

$2 + 2 = \underline{}$

$2 + 3 = \underline{}$

$3 + 2 = \underline{}$

Learning to Add (K.OA.1)

How many are there **in all**?
Write the number.

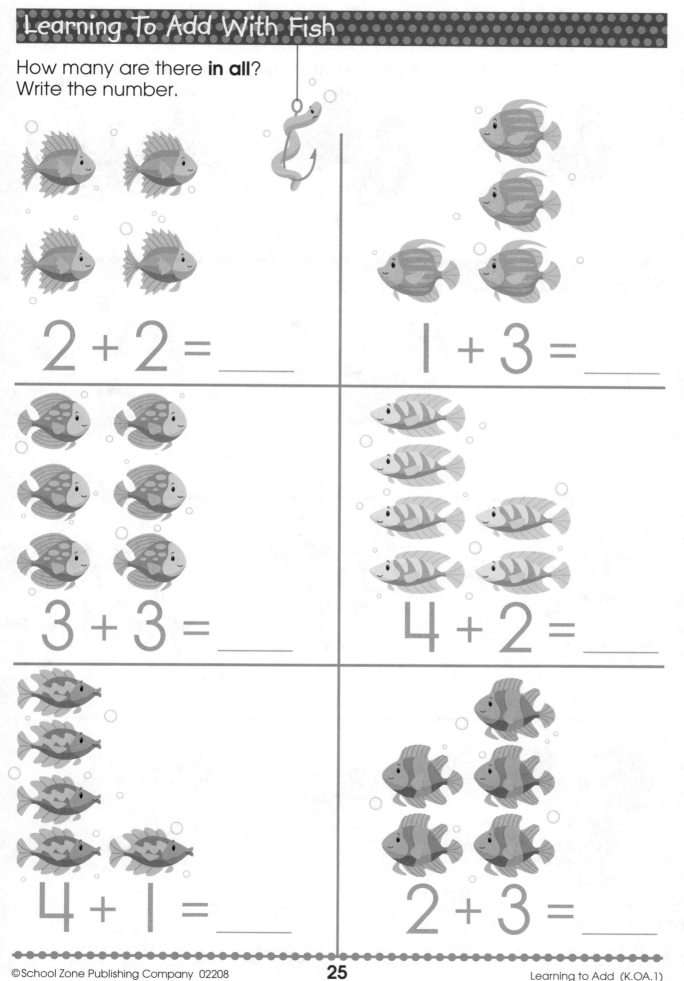

$2 + 2 =$ _____

$1 + 3 =$ _____

$3 + 3 =$ _____

$4 + 2 =$ _____

$4 + 1 =$ _____

$2 + 3 =$ _____

You can write an **addition number sentence** like this: $1 + 2 = 3$.

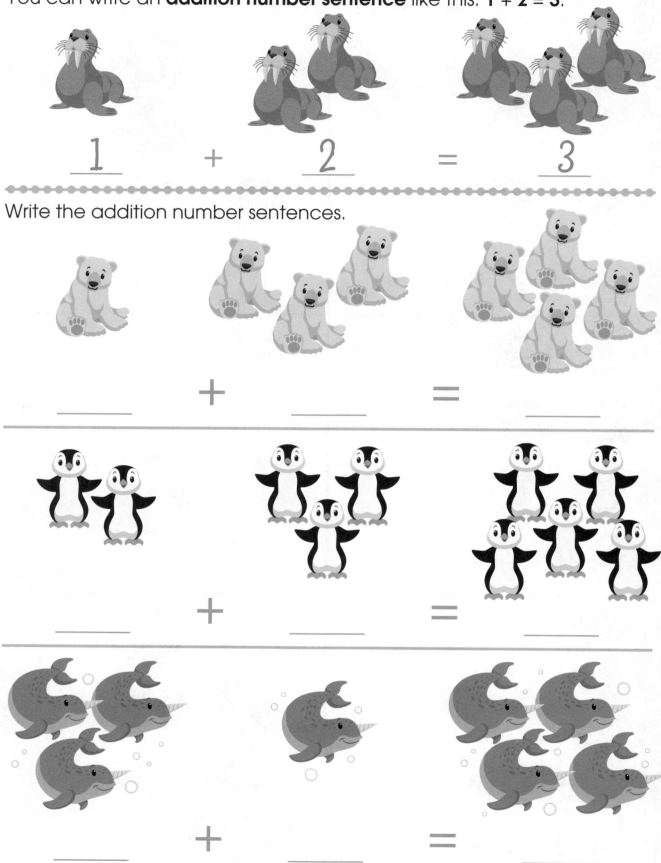

1   +   2   =   3

Write the addition number sentences.

_____ + _____ = _____

_____ + _____ = _____

_____ + _____ = _____

Write the addition number sentences.

_____ + _____ = _____

_____ + _____ = _____

_____ + _____ = _____

_____ + _____ = _____

How many are **left**?
Write the number. The first one is done for you.

3 - 1 = 2

4 - 2 = ___

5 - 2 = ___

4 - 1 = ___

4 - 3 = ___

3 - 2 = ___

How many are **left**?
Write the number.

$$5 - 1 = \_\_\_$$

$$5 - 2 = \_\_\_$$

$$5 - 3 = \_\_\_$$

$$6 - 4 = \_\_\_$$

$$3 - 0 = \_\_\_$$

$$6 - 2 = \_\_\_$$

You can write a **subtraction number sentence** like this: **5 − 3 = 2**.

5 − 3 = 2

Write the subtraction number sentences.

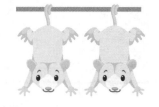 

_____ − _____ = _____

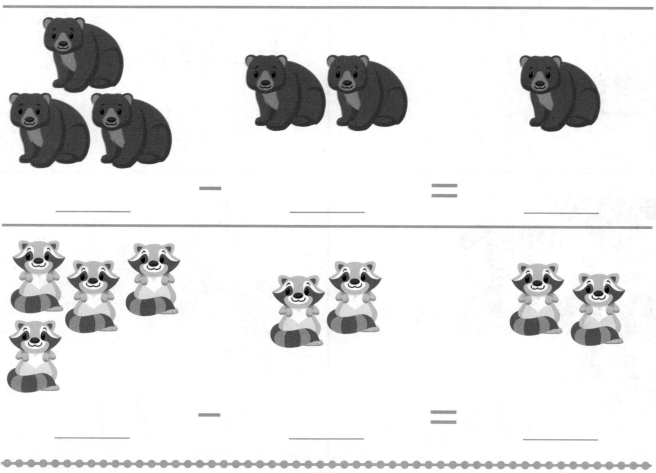

_____ − _____ = _____

_____ − _____ = _____

More Subtraction Fun With Animals

Write the subtraction number sentences.

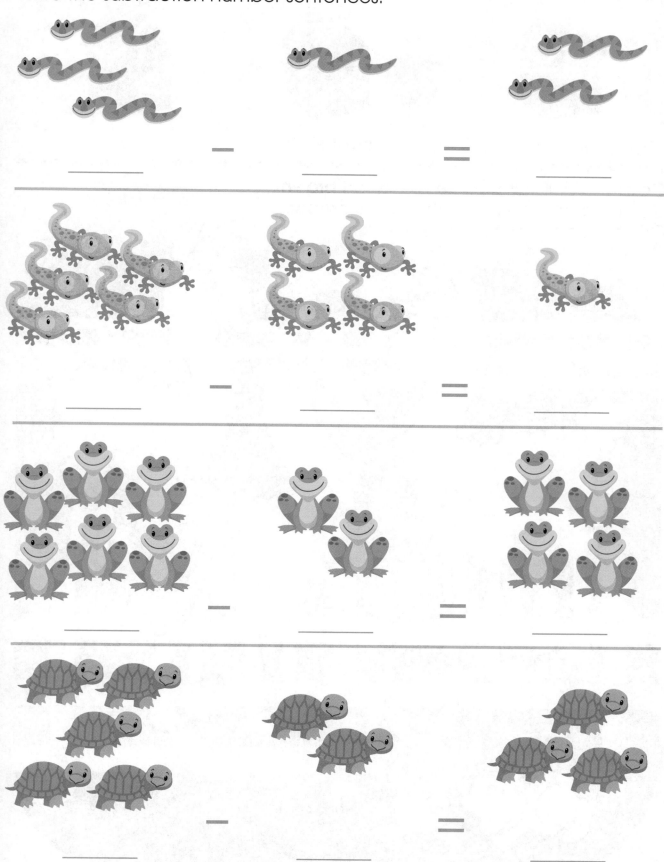

_____ — _____ = _____

_____ — _____ = _____

_____ — _____ = _____

_____ — _____ = _____

©School Zone Publishing Company 02208

Learning to Subtract (K.OA.1)

Where is the bird?

inside   outside   on

Color the animals **outside** the fence brown.
Color the animals **inside** the fence orange.
Color the animals **on** the fence yellow.

Where is the bird?

in   over   under

What is **over** the bookcase?

What is **under** the bookcase?

What is **in** the bookcase?

left

right

Circle the people who are going **left**.
Check the cars that are going **right**.

In Front And Behind

in front

behind

Circle the animals **in front** of the farmer.
Check the animal **behind** the farmer.

35

Learning about Positional Words (K.CC.5)

How many buttons are there?

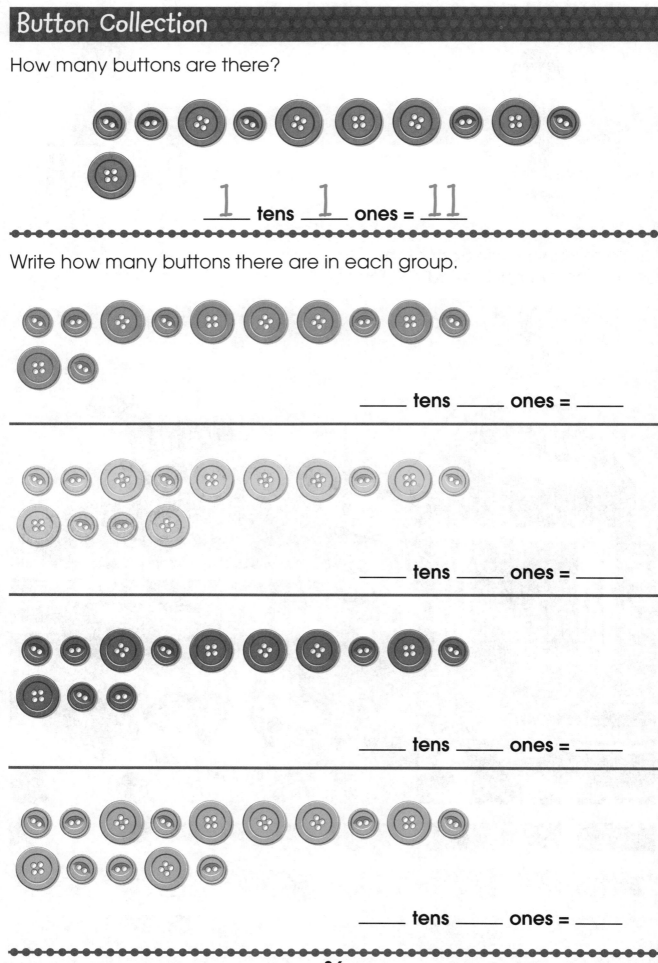

___1___ tens ___1___ ones = ___11___

Write how many buttons there are in each group.

_____ tens _____ ones = _____

_____ tens _____ ones = _____

_____ tens _____ ones = _____

_____ tens _____ ones = _____

How many buttons are there?

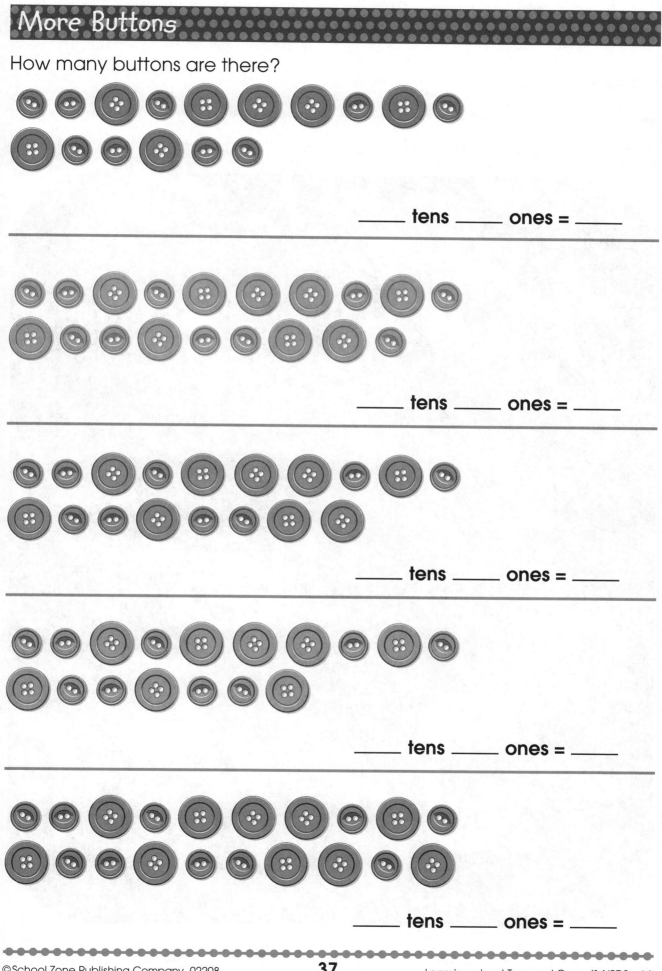

_____ tens _____ ones = _____

_____ tens _____ ones = _____

_____ tens _____ ones = _____

_____ tens _____ ones = _____

_____ tens _____ ones = _____

A **circle** is a shape that looks like this: ◯

How many ◯ can you find? _____

A **triangle** is a shape that looks like this: △

How many △ can you find? _____

39

A **square** is a shape that looks like this: ☐

How many ☐ can you find? _____

A **rectangle** is a shape that looks like this: ☐ or ☐

How many ☐ can you find? _____

Sides are colored blue.
Corners are circled in red.

4 sides   **4 corners**

Circle the shape with **3 sides** and **3 corners**.

Circle the shape with **4 sides** and **4 corners**.

Circle the shape with **0 sides** and **0 corners**.

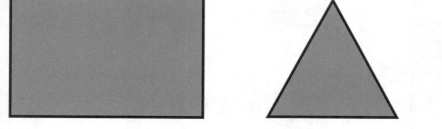

Making Patterns

Color the picture to complete each **pattern**.

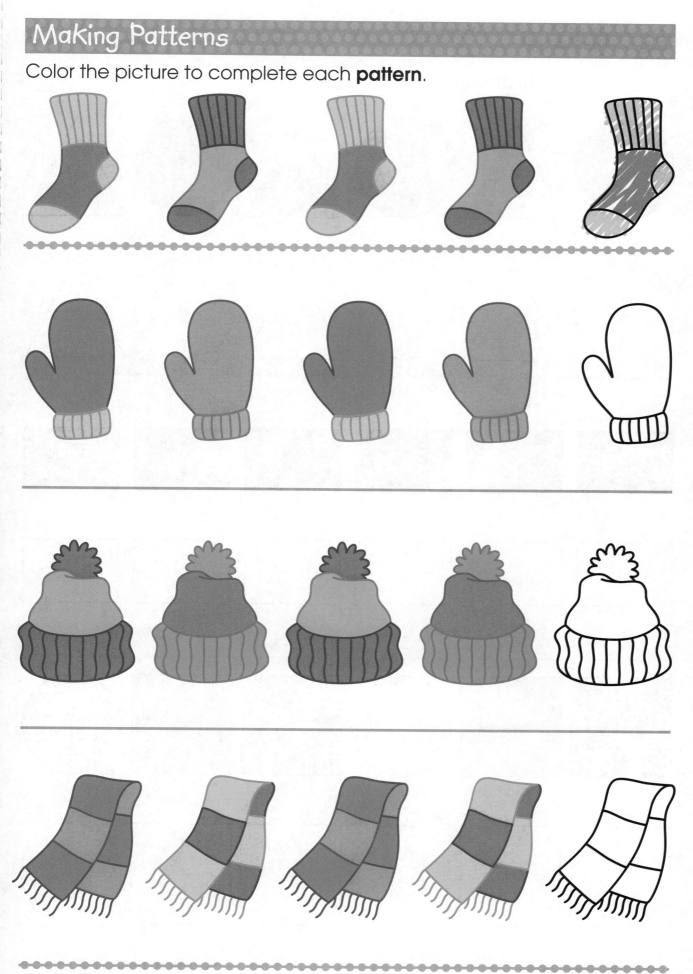

Copy the colorful **patterns**.

Shape Patterns

What comes **next**?
Draw and color the shapes to continue the **patterns**.

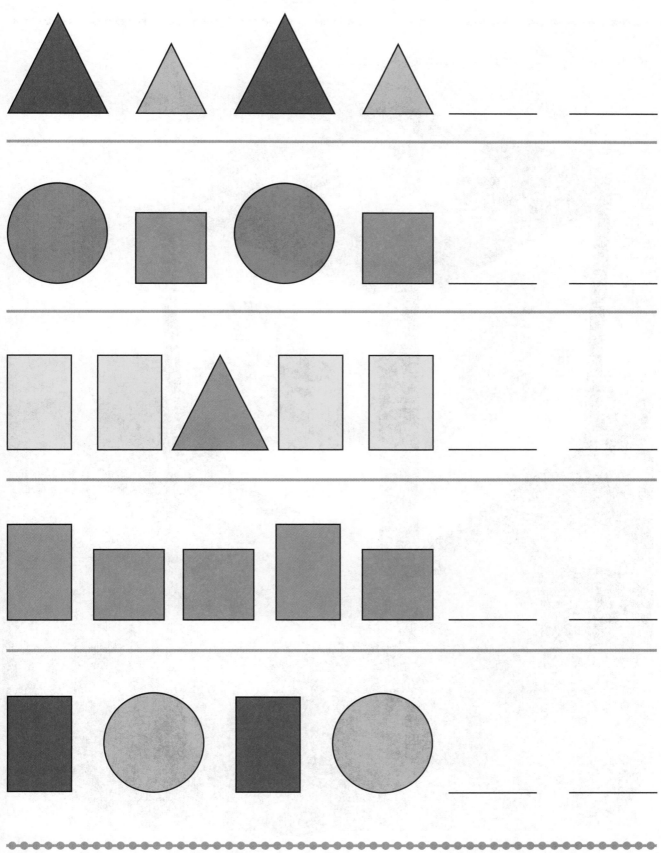

A **cube** is a shape that looks like this:

How many can you find? _____

46

A **sphere** is a shape that looks like this:

How many  can you find? _____

47

Solid Figures: Sphere (K.G.3)

A **cylinder** is a shape that looks like this:

How many can you find? _____

A **cone** is a shape that looks like this:

How many can you find? _____

49

Matching Figures

Color the objects that have the same shape as the first one.

Draw lines from the objects to the matching figures.

This is a **penny**:

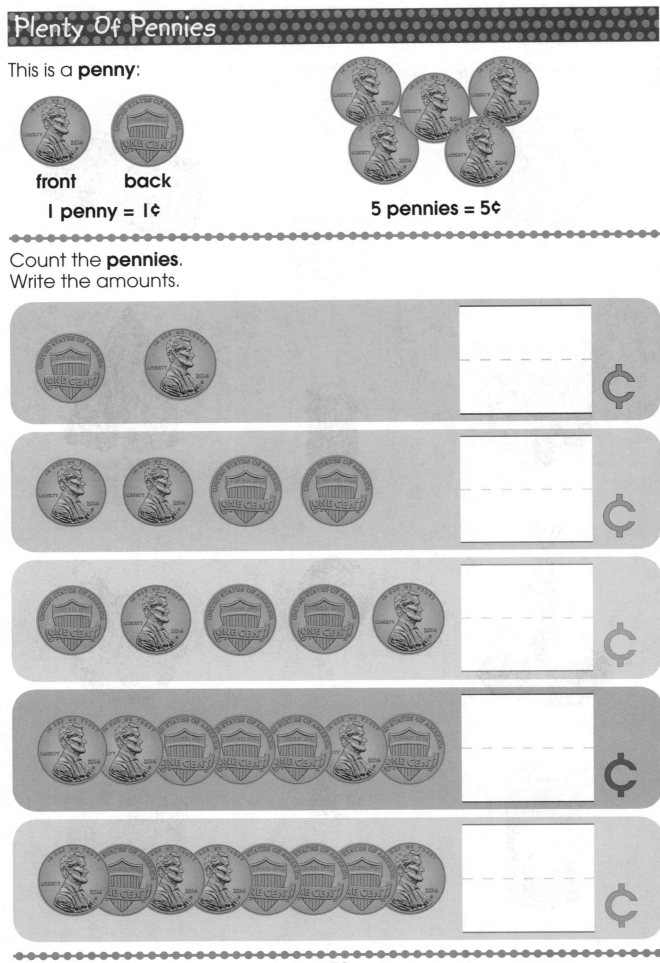

front   back

1 penny = 1¢

5 pennies = 5¢

Count the **pennies**.
Write the amounts.

Pennies And Nickels

This is a **nickel**:

front   back

I nickel = 5¢

=

5 pennies = I nickel

Count the **nickels** and **pennies**.
Write the amounts.

	¢

	¢

	¢

	¢

	¢

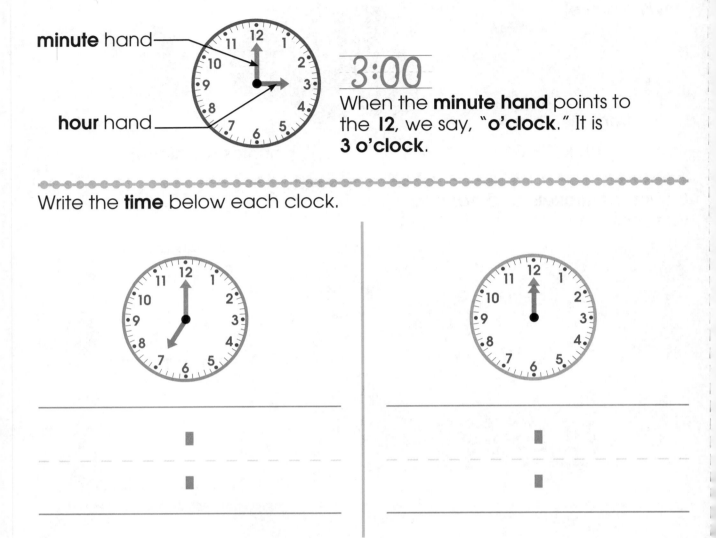

minute hand

hour hand

3:00

When the **minute hand** points to the **12**, we say, "**o'clock**." It is **3 o'clock**.

Write the **time** below each clock.

Draw the **hour hand** on each clock to show the time.

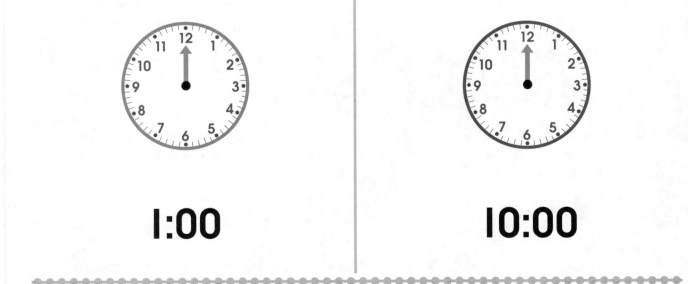

1:00

10:00

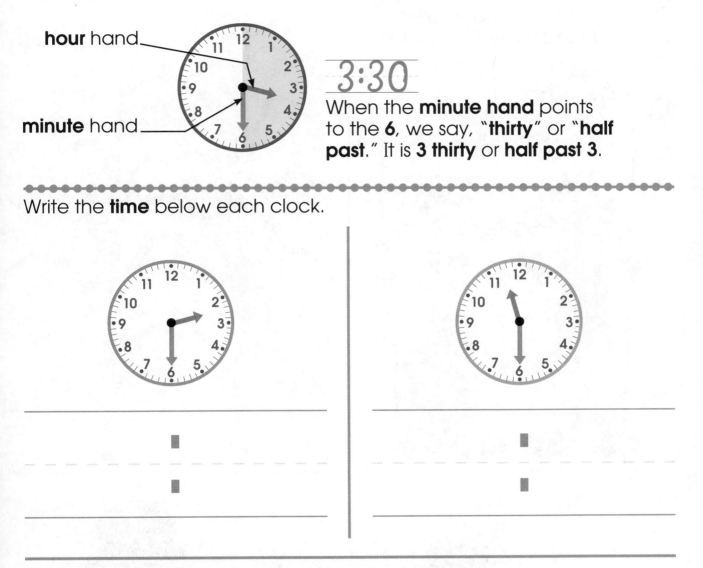

hour hand

minute hand

3:30

When the **minute hand** points to the **6**, we say, "**thirty**" or "**half past**." It is **3 thirty** or **half past 3**.

Write the **time** below each clock.

Draw the **minute hand** on each clock to show the time.

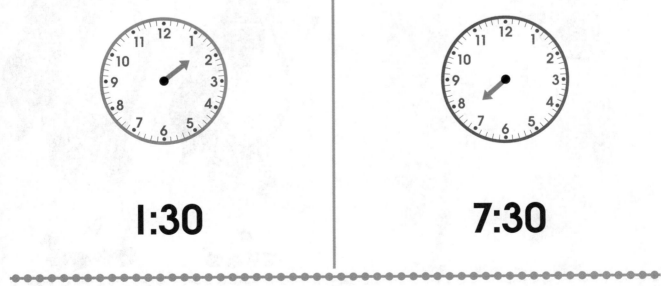

1:30

7:30

Check the picture that is **taller**.
Cross out the picture that is **shorter**.

56

Comparing Sizes

Circle the picture that is **taller**.
Cross out the picture that is **shorter**.

Circle the things that are **lighter**.
The first one is done for you.

Circle the things that are **heavier** in each group.

Comparing Volumes

Circle the things that hold **more**.

Comparing Volumes

Circle the things that hold **less**.

Match each picture to its frame.

Count to **100**.
Write the missing numbers.

1									
2	12						72		
3			33						
						64			
			45						
	26								
								87	
				58					
									99
10					60				100

Now count by **tens**. Circle those numbers.

GREAT JOB!
AWARD

YAY!

- - - - - - - - - - - - - - - - - - - -
Name

finished **Math Readiness**
from
School Zone Publishing Company.